I, Divided

I, Divided

poems

Chelsea Dingman

Louisiana State University Press | Baton Rouge

Published by Louisiana State University Press
lsupress.org

LSU Press Paperback Original

Designer: Isabel Webre
Typefaces: Whitman, text; Sabon LT Pro, display

Cover photograph courtesy Christina Deravedisian on Unsplash.

Library of Congress Cataloging-in-Publication Data

Names: Dingman, Chelsea, author.
Title: I, divided : poems / Chelsea Dingman.
Description: Baton Rouge : Louisiana State University Press, [2023] | LSU Press
    paperback original.
Identifiers: LCCN 2022058705 (print) | LCCN 2022058706 (ebook) |
    ISBN 978-0-8071-8017-4 (paperback) | ISBN 978-0-8071-8036-5 (pdf) |
    ISBN 978-0-8071-8035-8 (epub)
Subjects: LCGFT: Poetry.
Classification: LCC PR9199.4.D565 I223 2023 (print) | LCC PR9199.4.D565 (ebook)
    | DDC 811/.6—dc23/eng/20221220
LC record available at https://lccn.loc.gov/2022058705
LC ebook record available at https://lccn.loc.gov/2022058706

for Jay, who taught me. And for teachers everywhere.

A very small cause, which eludes us, determines a considerable effect that we cannot fail to see, and so we say that this effect is due to chance. If we knew exactly the laws of nature and the state of the universe at the initial moment, we could accurately predict the state of the same universe at a subsequent moment. But even if the natural laws no longer held any secrets for us, we could still only know the state approximately. If this enables us to predict the succeeding state to the same approximation, that is all we require, and we say that the phenomenon has been predicted, that it is governed by laws. But this is not always so, and small differences in the initial conditions may generate very large differences in the final phenomena. A small error in the former will lead to an enormous error in the latter. Prediction then becomes impossible, and we have a random phenomenon.

This was the birth of chaos theory.

—CHRISTIAN OESTREICHER, "A HISTORY OF CHAOS THEORY"

When a butterfly flutters its wings in one part of the world, it can eventually cause a hurricane in another.

—EDWARD NORTON LORENZ

Contents

ii. I over what was

iii. I over what can be

i.   I over what might have been

How to Live in Holy Matrimony

Sweat gathers between my breasts
       & thighs. Every morning, I wake
to heartache—

the lilies cry from dry beds. You say: *no life is without loneliness.*

At a courthouse, the justice of the peace witnesses us
vow to turn off the lights
& put down the toilet seat.

You say you love me.

You haven't yet handed me your heartache. Saw-
       toothed. Looming.

You aren't yet another version
of the lilies, lost to the ellipses between rains.

Consider the conditional *if.* What aches to be other than itself?

You used to call the rain
                 degenerative. Like any long sickness.

In some iterations, we don't know each other.
The rivers are lonely.
A life is all that's holy.

Fractals

As far as the laws of mathematics refer to reality, they are not
certain; and as far as they are certain, they do not refer to reality.
—ALBERT EINSTEIN

I married a man whose need is a mirror.

We had three children, and still this need
stares back at me from trees & coastlines

& clouds. The sea in my chest breaks
and breaks without fail. The paper walls
content our cries. It is night. We are lonely.

I married a man believing that some love lasts
the night. But there are other patterns

at work here. Hurricane season is upon us.
The children cry when he stays up all night

and tears apart the house. They are afraid

for my life. I rise and rise, the winds
high. I pull the birds' slight bodies into me,

cruelty the only country they've known.
I fear the rot the rainy season will leave.

In the retention ponds, a pattern is the wake

left by protected species that cannot flee. Past lives
hurricane in my head. No surface is safe

from weather. I'm careful. I take all valuables
down from the shelves. The kids' pictures

hide in the cloud on my phone, along

with whatever devastation that downloads
while we sleep. By now, I know how to be quiet,

to match the mirror's entitlement with a frame
made of glass. Where does any pattern end?

Rage is in the eye that passes over us. The kids'

voices are knives against the delicate beauty
of dawn. We find a room where nothing

changes, except the day. Dust on the bed
frame. The fury of rain on the windows.

We find a room we can't leave. But we can't leave.

Water blurs the windows again, wind tearing
apart our throats. I run my fingers over

the hurricane. It hurts where someone has been
forced to hide. I hide my children in my eyes.

I forgive myself for not letting them go outside.

Chronic Traumatic Encephalopathy

Small recompense: to lie anywhere under you,
the rain's broken alphabet
against the roof.

How to calculate the cost of living?

Tree roots conquer the sewer lines
below the house, forcing us to dig up the front yard,
filling the showers with feces.

You store memory in your hands.

Parsing the known from the unknown, you realize you are married
to a room like every other room. You scatter the years. Bury worship. Rough in
walls you put your fists through in the middle of the night.

You wear a hammer to sleep. The past
to leap from.

Mercy makes static of the world.

You might die. You might mean to. You might mean nothing
by anything that you do. Blame falls

from the edges of everywhere. But no one awards you

mercy

for breaking like rain against brick. For aching
the rain. The brick. For breaking.

Principles of Chaos

If the hurricaning sky wolfs
this sad peninsula. If depression is the glass
held up to all of this rain. If the rain
doesn't fall, but shimmies
against the panes. If rain. If brick.
If buckled, the brick speaks.
If brick is the language of our dead
cities. If we are left for dead.
If I kissed the bodies pulled from me,
more than once, in a hurricane.
If he is a man, is a monster.
If the brain cells that tell him to turn
a deadbolt turn the switch instead.
If the fire at the end of the switch
holds no apology. If he grew so sad
that I assigned him a hotline. If sea
-water needs. If the lilies in the front
yard overcome the leaves. If we can't live
this way. If lost, should anyone live
by force? If I said: *not in front of the kids.*
If his fist clenched. If my body intuited
the blow. If a hurricane, like a mirror, grieves
its center. If the sky, brick-less, holds us
here. Like that kiss held me, sick with him
as I was. If I don't remember light,
the mind an emptied drawer. If I must
hold him inside. Each cell wilting
in a field. If *fallow* is the opposite of *forever.*
If, in case this doesn't pass, the rain
is just rain is just rain is just rain.

At the Brain Injury Research Institute

What does your husband remember?

> Not the pain. Not the now of lists & memory
> loss. Not what his sons said yesterday. Not that we live as vagrants
> in Florida. Not that he called Alberta
> *God's country*, the frozen tundra sprawled beneath the sun like a road
> sign. Not his mother's cigarettes & wine.
> Not how she died, her mouth splayed open.
> Not now not now not now not—

When did you first notice the memory loss?

> What can I say about fog, except that it begins
> inside him now. That some beginnings are endings.
> That his brain turns us into secrets
> the way snow turns the world into afterworld.

Would it be safe to say that long-term memory is intact and short-term memory is where the deficit lies?

> Safe (adj.): 1. protected from or not exposed to danger or risk; not likely
> to be harmed or lost. 2. uninjured; with no harm done.

> Safe (noun): 1. a strong fireproof cabinet with a complex lock, used for
> the storage of valuables. 2. a condom.

How many concussions has he sustained in his career, to your knowledge?

> *782 lights line the roof of Joe Louis Arena*   he said   after his last fight
> what is the truth   if not a wound I remember as a heart
> -beat & he remembers not at all?

Tell me about his family.

What is a family? A fracture in the ice
over a lake? The feral wind. Hands
longing for a dollar, or diamonds, or a picture
of whoever we pretend to be in public.
Or is it how we've always been alone
in the world? The kids we might fuck up
if they don't understand where
they come from? The wind that takes
& takes what isn't nailed down?

How would you describe his mood swings? Any CTE symptoms?

Hurricanes nest in our backyard. Lightning struck
& caught the yard on fire during a monsoon last year.
Who says that lightning only strikes the highest point?

Have there been any changes in his appetite?

For sex? Or food? Or safety, when he is, again,
a small child that I coax out of the dark?

For another kid, amidst the panic of two kids?
This wolfish hunger that's his: for light, for asylum.

For a body to climb inside other than his own.
For this world to remember.

What treatment has he had up to this point?

Does wine count? Feverish night-rides through rain-
slick streets. Sleep, & no sleep. Rehashing two or three thoughts on a loop.
Sewing: the needle held tight, the pushback of the fabric

so like skin. Scrubbing tile floors to distill the weather in his brain.
But what human has ever been able to turn off the rain?

What are the most significant changes you've noticed over the last twenty-plus years?

When he says *love,* he means he can't stay here

like this. He means his hands shake all day.

He means he can't control his closed fists. The early

dark. Any god or human who condemns him as missing.

Or whomever, already, we miss, & miss, & miss.

Memorial Day

Not the storm, but the calm.
Not the flurry of attention
      called to the sky.
Not the rumor of a hurricane on the horizon.
Not the humidity, the mosquitoes rising
      like smoke from the fields.
Not a history of revisions we call
      love, or survival.
Not the children lost and discarded.
Not the borders that hostage them.
Not how we were once possible
      under this tyrant
sky, the familiar sorrow of the fields.
Describe our self-importance.
This awareness that travels us like a siren.
Why the live oaks drown in brown pollen
      gripping the streets.
Who else will wash this mess clean?
Laundry-damp, our houses.
Thick with spoiled food and loneliness.
In times of love and crisis, we've been
      the most alone.
Planes take off without us.
Children flit between namesakes like wasps.
We miss what is ours while it is within reach,
along with the dim sound of thunder
in the distance, storm drains already chuffing.
Let any absence mean we are loved.
Let the rain come soon and be done with us.

Litany of When

When the rain ruts the roof tiles,
when the palm trees say *surrender* instead of *sorry,*
when the winter here isn't winter anywhere,
when we can't absolve the sun,
when a fire burns blue, burns low,
when the ditches are burned, then drowned,
when disaster is a red light,
when disappearance is a shoreline,
when we call god by someone else's name,
when the dark is easier to earn,
when the only honest maps are made of skin,
when we're told enough times a woman is a curse
word, a catastrophe, a mourning ritual,
as we endure the chrysanthemums
furiously in bloom
here, the egoless red
ants, the rain that takes & takes
like rich men at a five-star hotel
bar, the world a thin waif
of a woman in the dim light,
a spell for loss—& what becomes of beauty
in ordinary light, I don't know—
don't we look happy, though, in the windows
of passing cars & rearview mirrors,
under the undulating sky,
the palm trees spread like canopies, & alone
we are, or aren't, or will be,
with the names of our dead in our mouths—: we speak
when we should listen, listen
when nothing speaks,
when this world is a lit wick,
when a flicker is all & all & all.

A Small Life

I don't know if there is a smaller life
to hope for. A river
passing the house. The fish
floating in the pit
of its belly, unmoved
by the water. Daisies
at the roadsides. The roads
without shoulders. The sun less
terrible somehow. Children
flitting in & out of fields
like a kaleidoscope
of butterflies, speaking
the language of wings.
And love is a kind of survival—
the river rushing past
that teaches the fields how
to pray. The small flowers
that erupt in spring. The butterflies
that feed on nectar & pollen
from the common milkweed.
Butterflies may only live a week,
moving from petal to delicate
petal, from field to sun
-warmed field, wings open to take
the sun inside, to lift them,
to hold them high, then higher
than need, than the green world
they've blessed with light, & color,
& the impossible beauty of wings,
of so many hearts, swiftly beating.

Powerlessness Is the Animal We Fear

In Florida during a hurricane evacuation, fuel tankers
drive I-75 South on *Good Morning America*

but never reach us. The gas stations empty, except for the lines. My son
drives station to station with me, his eyes bright as moons.

Later, bullets career through the bodies at Parkland High School. Amid after-
    threats,
our son's school is in lockdown for weeks. The kids sit through daily drills, not
    allowed out
of closets, even to piss.

We go to the beach for my birthday.
Another maybe-child spills from me like a constellation
        into the shower drain. At my annual checkup,

the doctors find masses in my breasts only an ultrasound can hear.

Tonight, the blood moon. And you. You call me terrible
                    names
as the hurt you've dragged over continents enters me like a picture-hanging
        nail, the claws opening a hole in my heart.

I dream all night that bars seduce most of the men I love.
The drinks, the drugs.

The prairie that holds our fathers,
                    we know not where.

The wildflowers I have already picked out for your mouth, river stones
        to cover your eyes.

I wake to suicide notes you leave around the house, on our phones.
Our son wears headphones to escape you, asking me if we can.

What I know is: we fell out of like, as he slept that night. The eye
of Hurricane Irma hovering over the city. The bay waters sucked back into the
    ocean
for three days before the storm made landfall.

So much of terror is in the waiting.

Tiny Initiating Events (the Butterfly Effect)

If not for rain, the roof would not be black with rot.

If not for wind, the children's bellies would not ache.

If not for depravity, I would not have come.

If not for the fires in the last city, nothing would be new.

If not for cockroaches overturned in the halls, our kids would not fear
death.

If not for hits to the head, a fist would not ball, would not strike again.

If not for the hand, the throat, the predictability of both
converging, one of us would not live.

If not for the wrapper I threw in a river when I was nine, the hurricane
would not barrel overhead.

If not water, then winter.

If not for a flag, the tree would not bow without touching the ground.

The littlest verb translated as action:
to set a fire, but not burn.

If the switch is a tongue, but I can't see the wound.

If the switch knows better.

If I once skipped with a switch, steeped in someone else's blood.

If no one saw, so all is lost.

If at all, I could care for the shoe or nail or drum,
touched once in another life, that keeps me bound

to this one. If at all it is fair that I carry the past in my hands
because I will die otherwise. If at all I beg you

to take it from me, so I can die otherwise.

Suicidology

i.

In some instances, the pines become prisoners,
splayed against the windows. Whipped
by wind. And us, trapped behind glass, yet

unbroken, like the skin of the crab
-apples fallen in the yard.
A threat is the flag

flagging on the neighbor's deck
as if deciding whether to lie down
when color carries

such weight. Light. Time.
Grace. And everything dying
here, with their lack.

ii.

      Test me
              not. Test me.

      Say *mercy*.
              Say it again.

      Which of us wants
              to be gone from this world,

      & which of us wants?

iii.

I petition the peonies
        to break less
ground, but inhuman they've been
        & I can't be seen through this
skin so I leave myself
        to the Illecillewaet River.
From the river, I learn
        how to empty of all
but fillings & filament, soul
        a makeshift parchment.
The heart, an exquisite wretch.
        Inside that water,
I lay down my worry, whispering:
        let this not hurt.

iv.

        —my love says he'll drive off a bridge with the car seats strapped
in the backseat   says he'll hit a brick wall with his head with his car
with his shoulder already shattered   says respect isn't earned
until someone survives what someone else cannot   says he wants to
    be draped
in a flag not this flag not this country not the country of his sickness this origin-
song   says his mother died to heal herself   says the wind stole his mind
says the arctic is gentler than the moon that refuses him
flight   says he gave everything so how much can he take & take & take & take

v.

See the wounded
       peonies. Their plight.
What lust has done.

       What I mean is: my heart
       is a well with a small girl
       curled into a sadness

       at the bottom
       who I've refused a rope.
       What I mean is: goddamn her.

vi.

Marriage isn't supposed to be composed
of episodes: the one where
they fight, the one where she calls
& he doesn't answer, the one
where the sky closes like a fist,
the one where the fist hits
drywall & shatters. The one where
nothing is the matter
except the fist, the light,
the mind a mushroom cloud,
& matter is that poor, poor sky
when so rarely we look up.

vii.

The weeds have sprung back again,
the ticks alight on the thick understory

near the woods. The deer stumble, unaware of fire
as half the province burns. In the province
of his heart, I survive like a child

whose parents are drunk all day
as the dawns siren on. The cherry tree

in the yard didn't ripen this year
& the raspberries appeared as pits
on the bushes lining the fence. Somehow,

I don't care if I never eat again.
The river, every night, journeys

through the future. Before, I doubted
need. Time's need to shatter all
that begins. Our human need

to deliver cruelty, as if our own
cruelty can be overcome.

Sentence That Ends in Sickness & in Health

Of course, the snow came again
as you forgot what it meant
to feel whole & half of the world
turned away, all color becoming past,
& I held my finger between the pane
& the flame reflected therein, moving
between moments of chaos & moments
where you didn't want to be found—
I'll be alive here even if you aren't, I said once
when you had fallen at my feet
in our bedroom, your back in spasms,
& I orbited that possibility, unable to fathom
the ungathering & aggrieved light,
the gaps between surfaces like bodies
in the quiet between trees, & how, each time
you touched me, I remembered myself,
younger, afraid of who I'd hoped to be.
Did I make you who you are,
or is the opposite true? I can't remember
the birds at that first house
with the constant rain, doors
opening to hurricane winds, & you
trying to escape the eye. When I am afraid
at night, I relive those moments
I spent alone, our first child in the bed
next to me, you lost in some other city or bar
or conversation that didn't include us.
Unthinking or undreaming, we came here,
to another country & snow,
to flakes that fell apart from each other, spiraling
like small creatures we could name
if only we had any imagination left,
but imagination requires energy,
& we'd had a third child that taught us
even the body tires of trying to escape

loneliness. New flakes feather the windows
like silent alarms, tonight, & I think that
I'll leave you here, with my next life
laid out in front of me: the trees
teeming with birds, I'll explain
to our children how rain against the roof
can be mistaken for laughter, & we were
loved once, & all you ever wanted.

Strange Attractors

To some physicists chaos is a science of process
rather than state, a becoming rather than being.
—JAMES GLEICK, CREATIVITY (2014)

Nights when we never repeat ourselves,
but repent the conditions of our lives
that continue to change while we wake,
while we sleep: chaotic is your mood
while living with brain injury, is my mood
while pregnant. The night forgets who it must
hold. All year, it arrives at different times.
Weather patterns change because of us,
but we protest change. We protest our patterns
in dynamic systems. We protest water only
when we are asked to drink it dirty. We protest
language when it causes pain. At one point
our lives spiraled apart, and then together.
I am reminded that my grandfather survived
wars and holocaust trains. When your brain
does not agree with your body, I dream
that train cars carry you off, the prairies
rank with ragweed and hay fields. I can't say
where you will end when you end. *Sundowning*
is the term for people with Alzheimer's disease
whose lucidity degrades by day's end. I am
a complex system swirling in the muck.
I am here to learn how to live without you.
Determinism has come to this: short-term
memory created recursively, a storm system
that repeats itself season after season.
Notice the way night destroys the lights
of whole cities in your mind while we sleep
apart, or together. How we are
conditioned to sleep through anything.

Deterministic Chaos

1. Some wars begin with butterfly wings

2. my heart, a katydid, abandoned in tall grasses

3. how else to explain love, except as a stock, exchanged
                inside a mother, a child, a suicide—

4. chaos means the hook & nail are near are silent are hung with care

5. when he tells me he'll kill himself, again, pale as the beaten sun

6. the river is an organ with the same gravity as a dying man

7. gravity: the crane with a hurricane shawl dangling from its neck

8. lo, the turbulent nights, wept & weeping
   lo, the child alone in my bed
   lo, the reasons my love can't articulate

9. the moon in its current position

10. isn't the point of life to help each other

11. live?

12. if revision is to re-see, what does the shattered body become
                when the eye receives it?

13. I've loved someone for more than half my life—

14. in abandonment, a door

15. where the future lies, broken;

On Traumatic Brain Injury

There are certain sounds that transform
  what we forget, what we remember—:

  the reassuring rhythm of the clock. The rattle
  of a fork on teeth. The mouth, petrified

open as machines *bleatbleat bleatbleat*.
The first beat of your baby's heart

  on a monitor. The flat line like years & months,
  long forgotten. The splintered laugh

  of a woman so like your mother's, except
  your mother is the almost-ghost

of refrigerator light in the kitchen
at midnight. And which sound or memory are you?—

  Are you the field swallowing milk
  thistle, hoping for a cure

  to the afterlife? Whatever did you need
  to be cured of: the disease,

or the mewling sound of your heart winding
down? Years later, I'm looking back

  at who you were when you were merely the sick
  crunch of snow under our boots, the lonely

  ache of the blackbird's call. I'm trying to tell you
  about the first winter without you:

the leaves have let go. Bare, the trees are
resplendent, like all things that we love

for what they lost when they were most alive.

In America

It rained, as we left that last day.

What did the trees mean
      to explain,

              bent as they were
      to the unruly street?

What did the wind speak
             of ordinary time?

Does anything left behind ever loosen
      from us? The string. The balloon.

The wrist. The sky that never stops
      moving.

We left childhoods, tiny
      galaxies, perched at the kitchen
      table.

We left with more than we had
      when we arrived.

What can we ask of time, except to forgive us,
      again, another moment
           & another?

Listen to the cicadas, all abuzz.
      The world, dark.

There is a moment in some future
      country, where we are uncertain

as snow. Yesterday, the wind called
        to the hydrangeas, each blossom
          loud & red.

The house, suicidal as a widowed bride,
                with child.
Tell me who we were
        when we first stood

at that door, asking to be let in?

Diagnoses

In this frigid winter of your forgetting
where any meeting is fragile,

        we meet between
morning & more snow. I picture
your mind filled with shadow. In some future, I hold

the skull saw, the light that the saw lets in.

Is it luxurious to be still
alive, after the life you've been given
                to forget?

Dementia gathered in my grandmother a decade
ago. She forgot my mother's name. Our faces. How she begged
my grandfather to take her home every day.

I can't imagine a cruelty that will allow us to keep you
             here. Stutter

of mind, stutter of hope. Should I shutter
your mouth to the wind coming
                off the lake?

In subzero temperatures, even the hares disappear.
The stars, like past selves, risen on dark water.

The snow kicked up by our shoes reminds me
of weddings.

How we eloped not once, but twice. Buildings
fallen in the background. The airports full of automatic weapons.

I'll try my best to remember
where we were & how & when, & who made who laugh
before the altar

of night, & how the cold snuck
into my hands when you were someone else, suddenly,

& memory was all that could separate us.

No One Can Tell the Bones of the Dead from the Bones of the Living

Not the dove's, its slick underbelly
           unfeathered in a wood. Not the winter

hares', their stripped fur like the exhaust
           of a thousand planes, strewn over fields

of ice. Not the diseased dog's, gone
           home to die on the carpet. Not

the depressive's. Debridement of the brain: bride
           from wedding dress. *Electroshock*

therapy still works, the doctors say. But the drowned
           man enters a cadaver

room, lies down in place of his future
           absence. He has never been less

sorry. Each day, his sadness is greater than any god's
           ability to stop it. Frustration is a family

unit, a disease undetectable except by sound:
           a cry, a deadbolt turning, the doorknob

reversed so the lock is on the outside. Try
           to lock any man inside a delusion, pale

as the horse harnessed to the field. Try to make
           the skin a permanent home. Pain

comes & goes only if the brain registers pain.
           In a family, one learns early to stay away

from windows. To stave the flies. That even
a horse gets spooked & runs

sometimes, the wind tearing through bone
like a child running for their life.

Springbank

Where confusion finds you, burnt-up
hangar, shackled to this vagrant snow.
Where we drive a snowless road. Where
winter lands inside you. Where we are lost.
Where little avalanches are known
only by the ground that moves
four thousand feet below. Where the west
used to begin & end with us. What skyline
did you hope to reflect? In your last fight,
I saw the twitch in your hand. The fist
driven through the bones in your face.
The cartilage floating free in the fluid
on your brain, I imagined. The tin
ringing in your ears will never leave
you. Hopelessness is a marriage of light
& dark. Again, someone you fought has killed
himself. Was the belt at his throat a religion?
Our heroes: bright as emergency rooms.
Who did you become while I looked past you?
Only the past remembers now. *Fight. Run.*
Train. All verbs meaning love is hard.
Hurt means *I feel your pain.* Where love starts.
Where in your brain the past aches.

Of Those Who Can't Afford to Be Gentle

after C. D. Wright

I say *coyotes*. As in, the shadows that follow me
in the fields. I say *fuck it*. By that, I mean:
in this age of isolation, I am tired

of being a mother. I'm not supposed to say
that. The mouths, open. The house in ruins.
And how is history any different? *Empires rise /*

people suffer / empires fall / people suffer. I walk
the same fields, asking the sun why it leaves.
Asking god how we can be so deserted

by someone we've never seen. There is a man
I've loved since my eighteenth birthday,
but we don't know how to be alone. Our parents

die in another country & we can't afford to live
here, to live there, or anywhere. Next year
at this time, I'll be in the same field. He'll ask me

to forget someone we've lost. I'll pretend
my shadow doesn't hunt. The sun will show
itself. I will suffer this age like light.

People will wish me harm. I'll count the days
I've been lucky. I'll kiss my children. All
midnights will add up to fire. When we hardly

matter, we'll revise our wills. We'll record
our voices. We'll pretend any ending is gentle.
The world, *made of everything and nothing.*

Topology

How it is to miss the particular loneliness of a past
landscape. One you left

because it might've killed you. How you want
that loneliness back

because it means that you do not have to endure
the landscape in front of you:

hills, strange with fog. A family that has taken on the shape
of sadness—all long O's, all mouths open

to snow as if trying to drown in a season
where drowning is scientifically impossible

without walking out onto a frozen lake and begging
something to break. How the landscapes

keep shifting beneath you, but not enough
that you notice. Even your own body is dense

with fog. Loneliness is what you stretched
your body around in Florida,

when you didn't know anyone and time was fragmented
by weather systems. How fear

and anger are now the seasons you bend to. All
deformations map the trials before.

You believe in the body. Or nothing. You touch
nothing to feel where it hurts.

You are asked to help others at all costs, but you can't
help remembering the lawn through the back

windows, the doe and her child that visited the yard
every afternoon, the streets brown with pollen. Loss

was whatever had drowned in the ponds while you slept.
Who can you help if you cannot

help yourself? Move forward. Move away. Move back
to the places where you began. Did you begin

with your mother, or did she begin with you? It's hard
not to tell landscapes apart, you are so changed

by them. Rise anyway. Your bones will hold. Nothing
is guaranteed to last and there is still time to go

where loneliness is easier. Where the streets,
like mouths, are not pocked by snow.

Even in an Emergency

You stand before me & demand attention.
It has been winter for years.
It has been years since I could breathe

    without fear. All of the doors flung open,
    spring will demand everything we have.
    Who am I to wish anyone gone

at a time like this? My brother, leaving rehab early.
The world, collapsing. Our children, friendless.
I was going to be someone else once.

    The world, ruled by weather, by markets.
    At the market yesterday, I was afraid
    of my own hands as they rose to cover

our daughter in her car seat. Where will we end
the year? It will, of course, be winter.
We will, of course, be lonely.

Epistemology

What does it mean to say we know the properties
of ice, of snow? The wheatberries piled in metal bins

in the silos. The house on a corner lot, properly
broken down, the septic tank leaking

into the closets for years, rats in the attic, box
upon box upon box of belongings that belong

to the long dead. Sex toys & pornography.
Money stashed in old socks. In ties. In tobacco

tins. It was once lovely. Flower boxes at the sills.
Large picture windows that held up the prairie

sky, faces of the parents we knew little, if at all.
How easily people end up like this, perhaps. We stand

at the tree line & I can't decide if "Mother's Ruin"
is an appropriate name for gin, or grain alcohol,

or every century where someone died, bleary-
eyed, a bottle within reach. *How do we love*

what is damaged? Ahead, the valley rivers through
the city. Ahead, the frozen prairie, the lone cross-

country skier. No one will find us here, I fear.
Here, the world is desperately bare. What now

is the prairie sky, if not another relic, burning?

An Incomplete Chronology

I almost remember the last world I left
        to look for you. Or was it to look

after you? The mountains, always blue
        in hindsight. The stars like streetlights

in some other galaxy. Beauty cannot return
        to itself, I've learned. I don't want

to go back to that world, but you've been sick again,
        in bed for months. I wander from room

to room, moving the chairs, a blanket, a wrist,
        to make anything rise. The sun has been kind

lately, but you don't notice. I almost remember you
        standing in the sun. What I wouldn't give

to crawl inside your body & work the gears. Now,
        you've been offered a way to return

to yourself. Back there: the body you crawled out of
        to save yourself from moving like your father

when he drank heavily & you were scared.
        I'm scared now. We've been alone in this house

for too long. Isn't there more to want?
        We hear voices in the distance. A dog barks.

A door slams next door & our house
        shudders. I don't know what I'm living for

anymore. Anything beautiful I've held
        too tight, I've crushed without meaning to.

Winter Solstice

The sun poses like a question
across the ice-covered lake.

Because the wind won't quit, I don't
        want to be held,

the panicked water quiet, the quiet
like a missing father.

When I turn to look,
winter is the gasp

from a poppy's mouth, the sky that won't return
to blue. I vowed to inhale

this cold anywhere your body sinks
below the horizon, below

lake water, below the silent
future we are so uncertain of,

as the sun holds the end
of this lonely year, where loneliness was

the least of our problems. The question
of snow in our mouths, here

we've been sorry, or lucky,
or loved as these last few hours

of light, where we've looked for ourselves
in the longest night, asking the dark

to come break our hearts,
to come break our hearts back.

Postliminium

I keep trying to explain faith, as in the mountain
pass that claimed my father's life

in a snowstorm. Or, maybe, I mean to explain

faithlessness: a blue that will not live beyond this sky.

Snow has come again to dull the afternoons.

One street leads to another, yet they do not remember
where they came from.

I've been trying to find myself in my body lately.

It's strange to be this young and this old
at the same time.

Where does the horizon begin and end when snow blurs
land and sky?

To say that I know how to be loved is to pretend
no one dies alone

when dying is the irrevocable task of the body.

I want to say I haven't been cruel.

Spring, in the distance, reeks
of the brand pressed to the calves' velvet backs.

My heart, splayed as snow. Wolfing what it can.

ii.   I over what was

While Reading Plato during a Lockdown

I see you everywhere. I see you
when the moon sullies
the hare's prints in the snow.

I see you in the windows
and hallways and eyes
hollowing my children's faces.

You might've been sick,
or beautiful. Everyone
has a father. There are few

words for loneliness
like a child's. I haven't slept
for so long. The night

shrieks like a woman
who wakes to find her
partner dead beside her.

I want to go wherever
sense has gone. All words
are injury: *sink, swim, kin.*

Did you hear the rain
last night? It fell
apart on the patio

floor. It fell to shadows
in my mouth. I'm asking
about death: like a star,

how it is to collapse.
I imagine you as light,
tethered to nothing.

I imagine I miss you
when I'm afraid
to open the doors.

My Husband Says Getting Traded between NHL Teams Always Led Us to Something Better

In Banff, it is snowing. Each snowdrop
heavy and wet as sound

when it reaches the ground. A man
reaches through the half

-light to make coffee, eggs & toast.
The ache of waking settles

in his spine. A future
surgery will be required. Today, the snow.

The house, quiet with sleeping
children. He is trying to find

a job. He is looking through the curtain
of snow. I wake & walk downstairs

to make lunches. Put strawberries
& hash browns on the baby's tray. We circle

each other, as if in water. The intimacy
of which makes us small. We say

nothing. We say nothing we mean.
We mean nothing, for a moment,

together. All assumptions aside.
We don't say: *it'll be okay.*

We don't say: *this is the hard part.*
We don't say: *we're unqualified*

for any other life. We don't say:
how lovely the snow. The world,

so bare. We don't say: *how lucky*
we've been in all that we've been spared.

You Were Found in the Belly of a Deer Once

Abraded, but clean. Someone cut you out, your face
purple, as if a panic of blood rioted there. You wanted
to hide. I know you did. The world, so painful.
You came upon the deer and crawled into the startle
of its mouth. You couldn't have known years
would pass and you would long for the leather
of the deer's stomach lining. The bones stripped
to paper by winter. The deer couldn't rise with the weight
of you. Two heartbeats to carry across rivers,
through the glen. Neither one of you could stay there
and live. Now, you are a grown man. Your wife has left
you. You crawled out of your life through an aperture
in time, wanting to go back to that dark place
where no one could touch you, where the dark
calls like a bottle you uncork so you can crawl inside.
The glass river you follow to find yourself, frantic. Even
in winter, water waits for someone to drown.
Yesterday, you crawled out of the bottle and back
into your life. Your kids stood at the door as you wandered
into the yard at daybreak. A bird, bulleting
through the air, had struck you. Against the door
of your heart, it exploded in fear. You haven't wanted to live
since we were little, though, have you? Little wind. Sullen
with morning. At your wedding, I held your daughter
under a sycamore tree. Then, I went away. For years,
I went away, while you sparrowed in the deer's shadow.
What is the difference between tenses? Before. After.
At night, still you visit the deer. Its carcass laid
to waste in the woods, blades of your blonde hair
sticking up through its bones. *Come back*, you'd said
when first I left. But I couldn't. I couldn't see
you without the sadness of the deer's dead eyes. Now,
I stand on your shadow to keep you alive. Your bones
caulked with whiskey and the circus wind. I would like
to tell you that there was never a deer. That you were found

in your room, the lights off, after our father died.
But you need to live in the belly of something
warm, without light. *Come back,* I say to the wind
that tethers the body to the lie. But there is no reply.
All I see are the eyes of the deer. Eyes that need
closing. The broken river that lies in wait.

Because We Can Never Know All the Initial Conditions of a Complex System in Sufficient Detail, We Cannot Hope to Predict the Ultimate Fate of a Complex System

I think I know the decapitated
sonnet you escaped from. The argument
without resolution is called *life*. Who

can survive strict forms stripped of an ending?
Acid & weed, then cocaine. Your body
another throwaway line striping tile

in a bathroom when last I saw you. You
did not speak but exploded into sound.
I want to say I survived our childhoods,

but I hate that I survived you. Little
brother, the sky is bright with surrender
tonight. Your hands are cold. The world flickers

in the distance. All that is left of time.

I Remember, I Remember

after Mary Ruefle

hallucinating the stars, like signal fires, as a man
convinced me to breathe in.

the mornings that I was low: the ugly
duplex, the cold basement, food stamps & clinic waiting
rooms where I went to get warm.

the way a mother's body is
                            softer afterward; a lived-in chaise.

the wind telling me *don't be afraid* as I let it break
inside me like a man.

the first poem I spoke was "The Lord's Prayer";
the first poem was the snow.

the loneliness of waking, the houses
still, & not ever my own—nor the hours, nor the years.

the mosquito in my ear canal at the lake:
        I had to wait for it to die inside me to be rid of it.

the first time I realized *woman* might be a male
construct—: the suggestion

of happiness: a pretty blouse, tight pants;
                                a short skirt, tits out.

the first cigarette, smoke like electric sand
-paper at the back of my throat.

the child that made my body stranger than the moon
in my fingers.

the child I was; she lives in the child I have, like a river
that seeks its beginning but finds where it will end.

the dust in the dark sills
                              that means I am diminished.

the day I let go of god, standing calf-deep in a lake;
my father was the dust, trembling against my fingers.

the three minutes I was dead in that hospital
room, the charcoal in my throat, my hair,

my teeth; I thought the nurse was the ghost
of my father, come to take me home.

the dead who don't remember; they won't stop
          talking about where they've been, about heaven—.

I remember everything.

I remember living. I remember dying.

I remember *dying to live.*

After a Suicide

The difference between who lives & who dies
      is the gauze of a moth's wing

as the tulips surrender themselves to the garden
      shade

& the sky fails to lighten this morning.
A father doesn't return home, his eyes

following small footsteps across the cold tile.

Tell me who you love the most & what you'd do
      to keep them alive, a poet wrote to a student

in a poem. The world is always half dark.
It is always winter somewhere.

Explain disease, my young son says, *how someone lives with pain.*

I never got to tell my father: *I miss you.*
He'd already been gone for months when he died.

To live, I need to make meaning of the dark
      again tonight.

What I mean is: I want to love the world
      as though it's something I'll survive.

Things I Never Give Myself Permission to Say

It's fall, & my mother meant to die. Gallons of wine & cartons of cigarettes
amount to suicide.

Reincarnation means that life is another thing to fear.

Here, war is a distant star that masses of people fall into, but no one sees.

Land, nor fire, nor chemicals have loyalty.

When I was nine, at my father's funeral, the priest said, *ashes to ashes,*
before we opened the bag and let him spill from our hands into the morning light.

What I heard was: *look at the sky. Heaven is on fire.*

I want to shave half my head & staple my tongue to the back of my throat,
but it would make too many people happy.

Barely fall,—I gave birth to my son as the planes hit the towers on TV
& I didn't know if I wanted him to live.

I am as far as invention and you are as far as memory, Susan Stewart writes in
      "Yellow Stars
and Ice." Am I the absence of loss? Or the loss itself?

My father said, *take care of your brothers,* the last time I saw him, sitting in his
      truck,
staring down the barrel of thirty-five.

The cattle at a ranch remind me of fathers. Their sobs as the brand bites into their
      flesh.

I keep thinking of what I would say to my children in a letter,
what words I would leave them with.

I was here. I loved you. Some days, it wasn't enough.

& What If I Spoke of the Hours

that we might've been together
at the union hall, with the beer

bottles & the night that didn't fall
away—. I might've saved you from

that car ride to the end of this calm

world. Would we have been happy?
The morning you died, I slept.

I got the kids up for school in the dark.
There were hours that I thought

you were alive. I keep thinking
about the cost of living. Your body

unwrung, & above me. Clothes
scattered like the hours you were

missing. What is happiness?
What I count on is the dark. The light.

Wanting to live anyway. The river
in my teeth & the reasonable grass

under my feet like someone I loved
once, impossibly alive.

Defensive Strategies

Tell me about the fog that became the fire that became the body. How you tried to rise above sky. The morning, crisp but wrong. How bodies fell from such heights. How, in death, anyone is indemnified. Or is it deified? Tell me about the song on the radio and the sound of engines failing. How the body is our greatest lie. The valleys splitting themselves apart in greeting. How the morning can go unrecognized. Tell me how anyone will live without you. How you were going to belong to us. How the sirens got further away as we waited for help. How help is nearby when the world is on fire. Tell me you meant for us to be alright. The fog rising to become sky. The morning, all wrong. How we rise to mirrors that will not remember. How fire touched you and you were lost. Tell me about fire. Police at the door. The sirens. How the radio kept playing, and we couldn't eat, and the sun refused to rise. How the neighbors collected on the driveway with food wrapped in foil. How the sun and stars will never die. Tell me no one died, and I will believe you. But come back from wherever you're hiding. The engine's on fire and the morning sirens through me. Tell me you forgot to rise this morning and didn't go outside. Just don't tell me time will decide what comes home to us and what falls from the sky. The valley, debrided. Your children, riddled with their own blood at a roadside. Tell me how all deaths are violent that aren't caused by time. Tell me why, and I'll forgive you. Tell me the authorities have it wrong. The fog, turning to fire. How last night was our last night. Your back at my back. How a body can withstand fire. How ordinary the light this morning at five a.m., the world rising to fog, then fire. How bright the hours of our lives.

Leap Day

We don't need to burn our lives down.
The snow, gone where everything goes.
Coquitlam. Maple Ridge. Hope.
That blue morning. You didn't come home.
I remember the god-awful lights
on the police cars. That no one lived.
Each year, an extra day arrives as though
time doesn't have a finger
on the trigger the way you used to
with a deer in your rifle sights. As though
the hunt didn't keep us alive. Were we poorer
then? We didn't have food or money.
The hares, in stealth, becoming snow.
The trees, asleep at dusk. Their hearts
pumping water to their bodies. All movement
within mimicking the world without.
It's been thirty years, and still.
What truths don't perish? Maybe we existed
for an extra day once. Maybe snow flits sideways
past the windows. Maybe something needs to die
so someone can feel. I've read that trees might feel pain.
The snow, a place where pain becomes ancestor to want.
You see, I should've done more to save you.
I say this not as a daughter, but as someone
who is trying to be loved. Next year,
none of this will have happened.
It'll be cold. Night will come.
The hares will have nowhere else to go.

Marcescence

What if death wasn't easy. The bathtub, full of liquor.
At some point, the arrows on the weathervanes
all point to another world. We should want to break,

not bend, I've read, but the boy broken over ice
in an ice bath is as lost as the air that trembles
his lashes. Accountability often looks like kids standing

on one side of a locked door. The sound of running
water. The banks drafts my dying brother called
promises. Somehow, I want him to stand ungrateful with me.

The leaves have held on this long: a dream retained
as the body retains a compass. A yield sign
doesn't stop anything from leaving. The streets,

abandoned again. Tell me how to lose someone
who didn't know he was lost. He'd already quit cocaine
& food, his eyes swollen to shelters. Why bother

with love? It snowed overnight. The snow's hush,
revolutionary. Estranged is water, midwinter.
I have no idea what any of this means.

After-wars

As crazy as your old man, they say, & he listens,
my brother, he listens when they say the world's
a soft & gentle place for a boy, but not this world,
when he tries to kill my mother, nothing hurts him
so much, when her boyfriend pins him to the fence
like a crow in a cemetery, the world can't explain the hate
that lies down in a man, a war that lies down in a woman
in a boy in a family, when he's the boy in the ambulance
& the ambulance driver, my mother laid out in the back
seat, he thinks the world is a hospital, each house
he passes housing someone dying, when he smokes,
it is to breathe like our father, & when he beats
my mother, it is to be closer to our father,
when he gets drunk, he dreams about being loved
like the world loves a boy with a lawyer or a doctor
for a father, he dreams he is loved like a bullet
that loved our father back, in the garage,
on his tenth birthday, when he dreamed he was
G. I. Joe, when the world wasn't yet the hurt
of a bullet, but a bunch of boys gathering
on the lawn to pretend they were soldiers,
to pretend that some soldiers survive.

Peripeteia

In this silence my brother bought
from the past: the suicides
of the aspen leaves in late fall,
our father's fallen shadow, quiet
with a future it won't cast, his body
bent over a missing country cast out
by new snow. A war in the woods,
time hung like a sheet between the lime
trees, handing down poverty that stripped our mouths
of language when we thought language
would save us. Even this page is depressing
for what it lacks. This snow, now,
so like my father's, the air silvering
with our lives, the little air he saved
when he didn't know a future without the drag
of smoke in his lungs, the click
in the back of his throat, the air trying to break
into flight as it escaped him. In the future,
there are few escapes. No one will wake, cured
of death, the moon uncaged. We might always be small
children, scattered at a roadside, searching
for our lives in tall grasses. The testimony
of snow trembles the fields, the grave
skies that swell around us like a pyre.
We've been running our whole lives,
my brother and I. Divided into ghosts.
The earth, razed or frozen into a haze
my brother becomes in the light
while I look past him. Some things
never happened. The blur of people
unmade. The paper echoes of the birch
trees in the winter wind. A secret war
shared with no one. The words
fired like flares into the night sky. The snow
ministering to the fields, even now,
as a river slips, constantly, by.

From Nashville, I Revisit the Days I Lived in Vancouver

How many shapes the dark takes—

my father, drinking at a bar near the train
tracks in the east end. 1985. A quiet suburb.
The leaves, shorn from the birch trees

by the river. My brothers & I waited

all night in the truck for him to come back,
the wind galloping. In downtown Nashville
tonight, I drink to forget how foreign

I sound. My vowels, winter full.

To forget the gateway of sky that hung so low.
The mountains held at bay by water. How fog was
a time of day. The two boys back at the hotel

that my father doesn't know. My mouth,

a warm cathedral. My body, my own. I drink
to forget the song a woman strums on guitar
strings. The melancholy wind. The three-day-

long rain. These labyrinthine streets.

How the many shapes of a mother are
like the hours: fluid. Indecent. Forgotten.
How suicide is the slow burn of a field full

of leaves in fall. How I smell them still.

I've never been able to say what's real.
The water. The woods. The soft grass,
softer than skin. The sad, solemn river

so far from its own beginning.

Psychogeography

where his body fell to earth like paper:
all that remains is a wooden cross,

wildflowers on the side of a highway.
I've been trying to go home my whole life—

my mother tracing my face,
my fingers. Trying to find my father

in the country he left her. I was home there.
Longer & longer, I belong nowhere.

Longer & longer, I belong nowhere
in the country he left her. I was home there,

my fingers trying to find my father.
My mother tracing my face,

I've been trying to go home my whole life—
wildflowers on the side of the highway,

all that remains is a wooden cross
where his body fell to earth like paper.

Noli Me Tangere

blessed are those who have not seen and yet have believed
—JOHN 20:29

My brother isn't ready to become the salvation
song stowed in an ear, the owls

spilled from my mother's mouth at midnight
as she sleeps four hundred feet from him

again. My brother: the quiet hush of snow
that breaks itself against the field. Helpless before

this blue hour, my mother uses her body
as a river. Water, even revised, knows

where it came from. My brother whispers
from his closet, mistaking it for a childhood

where abandonment wasn't the wild indigo that lives
through winter. No wound unseen will be touched,

but how to hold him as he dies again, my mother
on her knees outside her body. Tired of the heart

that cannot be touched without dying
a little first. That flat line. Electricity that begs

the wound to begin again. My brother, on suicide
watch, is unremarkable. But we are owls

perched on the brink of night & remembrance.
My mother loses weight to keep him

warm. To keep him close, we walk the city as he bows
to the myth in his cup. The news breaks

with a story about a little boy murdered
& fastened to a cross. In resurrection stories,

it is belief, not human hands, that brings anyone
back from the dead. We can't be saved

here. The fields of snow stretch under us. A hare
sits in the street, listening. Some ending seeks us.

What if this life is the only life we have?

Doppelgänger

If a saint & a liar are two sides
         of the same obols
we will place over your eyes,
         come time. If the drunk
& the boy go home
         hand in hand, one
a shadow stitched to the back
         of the other. If silence rises
like bile in one throat
         as the other chokes.
If the organs only fail
         in the drunk, not the brother
unsewn from himself in the quiet
         of his own burning.
If he isn't your only brother,
         but is half of a problem
no math can solve. If one integer survives
         subtracting the other.
If one looks healthy, keeps his job
         & wife & kids, pays
the mortgage as penance, puts food
         in his mouth, will the other
make fools of us as hope so often does?
         If there is hope. If, at all,
we have ten different doors inside us.
         What waits on the other
side of any moment? What threshold
         threads light through
our bones? Twining: the moon & trees
         through the windows,
the light with the living world.

Stigmata

Some of us are born to be our fathers:
        drunk spider in a drain, delirious
with water. Unmoored as a man
        who tries to smooth the lace
-edge of night from his face, to tell us
        he knows where he came from
as he comes through the back door, early morning,
        slurring his children's names
& birthdays. Our father knew this
        drunken fight in the clamor of pasts
we avoid, before he died young,
        a man none of us could know.
Now the question is how to escape
        biology, the bitterness of amber
liquid burning a black hole in the stomach
        lining, feet swollen with gout, veins
refusing to transport blood. Some fathers
        won't live long enough to be
martyred. There are days that I long for
        a perfect oblivion to carry me
to an alternate address, to trade wind
        for fire, blood for faith. There
are days I forgive this trope: the light
        that convinces us we know
where we're going. Our father used to say:
        you can be anything you want to be.
But we can't hope to empty ourselves
        of the past, memory, the miracles
scorning the lawn. Look at the trailer park
        where he tried to raise us. Where
we tried to raise him up. Holy, the dead
        in hindsight. Look at the way
the mind will shine any bankrupt thing
        bearing the marks of a life.

iii.   I over what can be

Shapeshifting

Wanting to be anything else, the sky
        disguises itself as weather,

& I hesitate to call myself *woman*
        when some man online says he wants

to shoot me dead for wanting a woman
        president, the scope of his rifle

an argument I will finally lose for lack
        of language, however much I refuse

to believe that language doesn't hold all
        meaning. I refuse to be that passive

willow standing in a field of snow, the blue
        horizon surviving below-zero

temperatures. I refuse the stink of future days
        like a wound, open & unclean.

I refuse the long hallway in the past of pasts
        where I wanted to be the fury

of wildfire, the devastation of the uncontrolled
        burn. Control is for the weak, god

-dammit. Last year, a man ordered me to go
        do my job, by which he meant

go be a mother. My ovaries, in bloom, ached
        with their own weight. I was teaching

four courses, running youth sports programs,
    writing. I already had two young children.

Some things will never change without a revolution
    that ends anywhere but where they began.

Apostasy

The religion of the body
I no longer agree with. Waking

in pain, I can't locate
the source. In an ultrasound

room, dim-flowered as a spa door, I
uncurtain. I wait alone, thinking

of a strange dream of men I had
last night, their thumbs interlocked

as they passed me in cars that floated
down a river. Their faces were closed

fists. *I don't believe in pain,*
my mother said, the first time

her body failed. In another room,
I lose control. I end every sentence

with NO. Why do most attacks
come from within? I've been

a loyal follower. I followed the pain
to its source & found only this

dull reason. A system of cysts
on my left side, this machined galaxy

emptied of doors. A kind woman
presses her hands to my chest,

asking, *are you okay?* The pain,
a garden of weeds that sprouts

into masses through my ribs.
For everything this body has given me,

it takes & takes: a yield of innocent
lives. A promise to wake.

At the Insight Ultrasound Lab for a Breast Cancer Screening after the Mammogram Finds Irregularities

Imagine this:
white petals spilling from the walls.

The breast over the heart, exposed.
What can enter the heart, what cannot.

A family history without cancer.
Where I'll be in a year. Where I won't be.

The sound of the ultrasound machine, ticking
over each bombed-out cell. This room,
the gray scale of a treatment center.

How technology breaks the body
into pixels. Into patterns. Into dim light.

My husband, not allowed in, waiting outside.
The hand that writes this. The wait & weight & wait.

The quiet before our lives change like the seconds
before a wreck.

The body's wreckage. The beauty of it.

This record as archive as testimony as trivial.
How we'll tell our children. How we'll be remembered. How?

It was once thought possible for people to fly.
Heaven is a place I can't imagine.

All the years I hated my body. The mirrors. The life it has given me.
A reason not to mourn. Any reason.

Us, together in future photos,
our bodies silhouetted by the sun.

As Stars Burrow against My Ribs

This bright morning unsayable
as the sentence of the woman who died
in daylight as her children climbed her still
body in a hospital bed. She left video
messages behind. They cry now, & I feel
the cells under my arms tighten with ghost
-milk. I feel my breasts for cysts
that have spread into a map of the next
world. *Will I live a long life?* is all she asked.
No one answered. I used to scream
into the woods behind my house. After
my father died. As my mother felt her cancer
spread. No one looked me in the eye.
No trace of the stars in the morning
sky, the mind still hungers the problem.
The night has flown from the pines. Wind,
arguing for centuries with the trees,
is elsewhere amazed at the hawk's dive.
Unsure what my body is built for, I starling.
I blacken the edges of snow. I let
my children down, starlight on my tongue.
The cells like dark stars refuse to die
on my left side. The last biopsy was
elegy. Unsayable is all that I imagine.

Apophenia

When *mass* isn't a murder, isn't a black hole,
isn't a service, but a secret army of cells
that multiply when they divide. Here,
this need for connection. The shape & color
of the wound as an answer. The woman
laid down in the snow like the outline
of a ceasefire. The posture of my mother
as she must've prayed, the tumor
a small tree growing in her lung. *Now
I lay me down to sleep.* The masses strung
together in my breasts, I dreamt, as a thousand
paper cranes. *If I should die before I wake.*
The power lines as they ascended the sky
from the window, my mother dead
in her hospital bed. So near, but so far.
The morning, gray with birds. The maybe-
god that lives inside each of us. The violent
difference between *keep* and *take.* Today,
the bitter cold that climbed inside my chest.
The sun so bright it stopped me. I stood
on the path by the lake. I wanted to run,
but I couldn't. The pain in my chest
exploded into a thousand bees. But I was
warm, for a second. There. Still-life
mimicking the next life. Or just the sun,
as it laid itself across the lake. And
I was tired, suddenly, of having to pretend
that mass murder is not a disease.
That a service will not be the end
of another life. *I pray the lord* to save me
from myself. Perennials recreate themselves
from holes in the concrete. From cells
in the body. From the aftermath of snow.

Hear the weeping of the glaciers.
Hear the bells inside the river inside
the wind. Hear the wind. Its laughter.
Hear the small white lady's slipper,
immobile, keening in the midday sun.

Praxis

To orchard the blood.

To goddess the cells
    inside or outside the body.

To strip-mine the lobes thick with tumors.

To mobilize the injection sites.

To swallow lamplight, not sugar.
    Not caffeine. Not the hanger
    hung with the suit they will raze you in.

To cannibalize the marrow.

To harrow the hours when no one comes.

To come, but not apart.

To symptom the problem of breasts, of body, of being
    born.

To woman this acre of history.

To story the child.

To child the years with new hope.

To hope: the fireplace lit in your bones. The bed next to you, unemptied.

To say *age* and mean *disguise*.

To halo the swelling.

To flaw the future like a long winter in the fields
     defiled by crows.

To winter this wanting to be alive inside.

To whisper, *I won't let anything hurt you*, into the wind,
     & fear not what you'll have to survive.

Complex Nonlinear Systems

I walk through white hallways, all
leading to rooms where people are told
whether they will live or die. The cysts in my breasts
may or may not kill me, but I will learn of them
on the same screen that holds my daughter
in the uterine sac, her profile
hawkish. All things are imaginary
until we can touch them. I am touched
outside and in. The technician
runs a wand over my belly, my breasts.
If not for the fetus that I mistook
for perimenopause in my early forties,
I wouldn't have discovered the potential
for threats that live just under the surface
of my skin, as though a thousand
ticking clocks. Some women
say fertility *ticks* inside the body,
but I've felt the end of time rise
like lost letters that no one will ever find
since I was a child and all was dying. Everywhere
that the wand travels, pain
follows. I swallow the urge to cry out.
I will wallow when there is reason. In this room,
the walls are dotted with butterflies. Real
butterflies have a life span of one week.
My daughter is trapped in the chrysalis
transecting yesterday and tomorrow. I need her
to live longer than a week. How I will survive
after she leaves me, I don't know. Barren,
perhaps. Stripped down to the teeth.

When the Right to Life Isn't a Right

Forget the flowers. The fact that despair is all
I am tonight. Forget assault, washed clean
by the moon, the debrided miles. Forget
the mess of carnations in the grocery store
aisles. Their wild cries. Forget I am alive
& the cluster of cells in my belly are new
enemies of mine. Forget that I've wanted
a child since I couldn't carry one to term.
That a fetus can die by accident. By rhyme.
By way of an inhospitable uterus. Forget
the test I took at ten weeks to find out
if my baby would be born at all. Born alive. Born
without a life-threatening condition. Forget
the young doctor who said *everything will be*
alright. You have lots of time to decide. Forget that
I lived in another country then. Forget
I love. I feel. That all can be forgiven. Forget
the names for children I hide inside a lockbox
under my tongue. Forget I can be prosecuted
in some states if I lose another fetus. Forget
the fool tides. Forget the alley I might die in,
in another decade, another day. Forget this moment
exists not to save lives, but erase them. Forget
the bee populations, dying as they pollinate
the flowers you'll cut down to bury another girl-
child. Another child. Another's child. Forget
the body that was once mine. Forget legal
bullets that cut children down. Forget where
those children might be now. Forget who. Forget
the violence in our world. In a word. Forget that
women & children have obeyed the laws of men & nations
& states to find ourselves unsafe. Forget how
we've always been unsafe. Forget: at six weeks pregnant,
a woman may be symptomless. Forget the science.

Forget what the body can and cannot abide. Forget
that women are told that a fetus must survive,
but not how to survive this lie. Forget the way men fall
down inside a lie. Forget anger as unjustified.
Forget swearing off sex or pregnancy or pleasure.
Forget that a leader's riflescope is largely unused.
Forget it is the soldier's duty to peer through
that aperture & pull the trigger. Forget
who will die for this. Forget who will be forced
to live. Forget how. Forget the lye. Midnight
walks off a bridge. The coat hangers that will tear
new apertures in the wound. The wound
that may have a heart. The heart that may
beat. That may or may not beat like mine.

Occupation

This isn't love, I keep telling myself. The body,

an interrogation room that I will never leave.

I used to be magic. I conjured leaves from a grotto

to compare levels of pain. I starved myself

sightless. I gave up all that I knew of being a woman

in order to be loved. I refused any answer

that began with suffering. I pushed my body away

when I was afraid. You were close to me, then. You watched

as I fell from myself when I couldn't keep other people

alive. I conjured a body that kept you near. I have to tell you:

nothing saved me from believing in the future. The photos

gathering time. The bones assembling me. Like fire,

the body may be indivisible, but only if we love it

a little. Here, the enemy of the state is the new child

who sleeps in a swing next to me, the morning

breaking in through the windows. The truth is:

I don't think I'll ever be enough for anyone.

The truth is: it shouldn't hurt to be held.

It's Possible Sex Is Elegy

You're making an argument about sex—
yours, theirs. Whoever sorrows up your sails,

shitty with dead mosquitoes & smoke.
You want to hold your body against them.

Break the sound barrier. Cut your bangs with
a butcher knife. *Say everything you can't.*

Who doesn't want to say what can't be said?
This body is mine. This body, uncocked.

Still, they say; there's no argument outside.
The wind is low. The oaks, stripped & solemn.

You've quit pretending that love is the point.
But you want. You storify & woman

& weather. You break your breath against sky—,
on nouns, human, & close, & not enough.

As Safe as Night

After   he tells my friends   how awful I was
how I laid there   unwelcoming   *where are we fucking*
going he'd said   as if he deserved all doors   flung open
another gap-toothed prayer for beer   instead
of food   instead of forgiveness   as I strained
to hold myself inside   the tree limbs   stitched
with sky   as I strained to believe that I was ever
young   that girl   sick with the wind's exorcism
the moon   slutting   in a valley's gullet
a man's mouth   on each word   I couldn't save
for myself   the dawns that arrived like shame
to settle in the trees   I've said nothing about
that night the dark the trees the sharp glancing pain
that came & came & came   how I couldn't stand
on my own for hours   or was it years
my body   mulched   mistaken   for an invitation
an entryway   I shouldn't have had to enter
this story   alone   this sad this sorry   starved
lash-less   I've never made a wish   on anything
I've lost   I wish instead   for a night
that could be safe   from all this dark

When the Wind Culls Its Name

from frost laced over fences and ferns,   there is a fragment
of past tucked inside

the meadow. A sense that I've been here before, yet
I didn't know what it was to loathe the quiet

a body is owed.   Somewhere,
in these lean months, survival reduces the ragweed

to nothing.   The first time anyone touched me
wrong was the first time. Near any home, defiled

is the snow   stone   fence.   Above,
the planets beg to be known. Who pretends to be alone

when touched?   The body, in all of its quiet
escape.   I'm not special, but what does that matter

when bone turns to night?   Midnight
trains pass through the country

of my waking and, more than this cold,
more than the specific quiet of the unknown,   to strip anything is an act

of tenderness   rather than a tell—
did I ever tell anyone   I'm not comfortable being touched

or did I let the world enter without using a door
in order to prove what I'm willing to surrender?

What is surrendered: the night, put down
next to the fence   the body   the whereabouts of a blizzard

that buried itself in the woods behind the house. Blue
was winter. I was once. Even now, the snow   I fell.

Here, the Sparrows Were, All Along

Every minute or so, a hallelujah
dies in someone's mouth. Every minute or so, a gunshot.
            A ceasefire. A tire shreds

on the highway, & pieces flit like sparrows
across the sky. Silly me. I thought
            we were here to live.

The garden's hallelujahs: tulips & rhododendrons, alive
in the ground. We expect so much
            of life. Once, I was a child. Then, a child

was locked inside me. Now, a different
country claims us. Tie my hands
    to the wind. Strip my mouth of any country

                    that doesn't fit. Sorrow the sparrow's
steel cord & textile torso. Its irrational wings.
            The problem with flying is most people

settle for land, no matter how often
we are unloved by land.
            Rewind the centuries:

before planes, the accidents of a gun,
or mouth, or gentle morning, how many people
            believed they could fly? Breaking gravity,

what names did they cry when they took that first step
away? Listen to me. I'm telling you
            what only the wind knows—

here, the sparrows were, all along. Nailed
to their species. Alive, or not
            alive. Sometimes, not alive at all.

Notes on Inheritance

When I see wax, I think of submission.

I think of afterlife. I think of the sky
& what it leaves behind. I used to think

myself a doe, then a hurricane. The muscle
inside the tongue. The prayer-sore. Again

& again, something foreign. Fugitive. So briefly

I was a girl. A young woman. A mule, mother, arm-
rest—the sky resting on a bridge overlooking

the river. That cold, cold water. I waded in,
three seconds to numb. & nothing. I can't give in

to love. What will become of us

when it's the child that is imagined?
Our gods: the fields under a haze

of mosquitoes. And lo, the stars' white
fire. And lo, the splintered spines of spruce

trees. And lo, the disappearing hours.

I stretch my neck into the next life.
I breathe in the cherry blossoms & bomb-

scent of aftermath. I don't care why

I didn't want this. I lean into myself.

I take what is offered until I forget

I am what is offered. With the orchard
& the apple I didn't name. There is

an hour that bears my grave already.
It's late. I can't help but wish I wasn't

lonely. That I wasn't made to disappear.

A Name for Illness I Knew, but Couldn't Say

—after Jennifer Chang

What if.

        There is some guarantee
        of safety—: the light,
        ordinary & near. The future,

a wind that spans the river as the swans
float by. No winter in sight.
No sorrow. No moon, consumed

        by prayer. What if where we are
        headed is nowhere special?
        Like the herons that strut

through the neighborhood. Slow.
Nowhere to go. Inevitably, back
the next afternoon. There is no plot in this—

        it's colder at night than I remember.
        Tell me, dear sister, where did we part?
        And how did your body let you

down? Your brain on fire.
The tumor that made nonsense
of our faces. Face it: the shape

        & texture of the night doesn't matter.
        There, the bridge. The cicadas.
        The forgetting. The starved *we we we*

wailed by the warbler. Stop me
if I'm wrong. I wanted a future full
of tequila shots & gutrot—all the wrong

        things. It wasn't until the thin of you
        was whim & calcium that the herons' need
        to walk toward any skyline meant

we had lived. And love is like this.
Too much or too little. It's late
now. We'll never be loved right.

In the Alcoholic's Apartment, a Time Machine

Your mother is dying for real this time. You say
coming home is like breaking the bottle in her hands

& swallowing the shatter. I sweep up the glass. The rain
comes early, morning cool & calm, but ever

-gray. You want not to stay. You came for your name
& the names that grace her mouth like a favorite

chardonnay. In this exhale: the cancer in her spine & lungs
& lymph nodes that she hid until it was too late.

Is this escape for you? Slow death. Guarantees.
I marvel at the bend of your fingers, the old costs

of living. May you not blame the boy you left
in a gold-plated frame on her dresser, the shitty apartment

she saddens, the bottle sweating next to the ashtray
on the nightstand. You want an apology, but there is only

disconnection: a cord from a body. The body from itself.
In any homecoming, what can we do but echo & ache?

To leave ourselves as one thing & return as another?

It's Possible a Mother's Body Is Elegy

i.

I stayed away until your body was
a rumor on the arid summer air.

How I wish I'd given more thought to death.
To the windows that kept out more than cold.

To the black-silk morning where I left you,
quiet & ashamed. Can anyone do

without all of this humanity? Stuck
elevators. Cracked glass. Earbuds torn from

someone's ears. The habits of the living
that leave me lonely now. What shall I love

instead? I remember us, here, the maps
of our bodies brilliant & loud. *It's time*

to go, you'd said. The truth is a steeple
I can't enter. Bells I can't hear ringing.

ii.

I can't enter—bells that I can't hear ring
like birds that will be killed by the windows
I shine so I can see myself inside
something that will last. The seas hold bodies
I will give away with clouds & light. Trees
know better than to move, except slowly,
as they migrate west over years. Here, there
is nothing I won't die for. *Silo, wood,*
lasso, tornado, grass. Mother: who isn't

afraid of the glass & what we see there,
staring back from inside a body we long
to keep? Dear woman, dear sovereign, what life
have you forsaken? How I loved you.
And now, what will the world do without you?

iii.

And now, the world will do without you. Rain
again today spells the end of language,
of the body, of all we don't know about
living. You never woke with spit in your
hair, pulled from bed by light. Forgive your hands,
your tongue buried like a bucket in time's

well, the way you flinched at the beginning
of wind, the sky moving so fast you broke
your teeth on the clouds. Here, Mother, you've been

every woman to everyone. Quit being
so polite. Politeness killed the river
trying to break free of the yard, run-off

from the storm gathered in its quiet mouth.
There isn't a woman I believe in now.

iv.

There isn't a woman I believe in now.
You are a cistern, a sense, a silence,
& this sadness is not new to you. Spirit
-less, homeless, less & less a person who

set a field on fire to see something burn,
who buried the wind in an acre of sky,
who carried every person you've known on
horseback over the prairies, east toward

the seas you'd never seen, only to be
unable to drink from them. If *a word*
is elegy to what it signifies,
"water" means we have little we can hold

long. Sorrows are the children at play in
the fields, like lesser gods we'll grow to lose.

v.

The fields, like lesser gods we grew to lose,
        lit with fireflies at night, & you not yet

a mother, not yet other, not yet shape-
        shifting past. What made you important

before my wings' vibrato inside you
        made you imaginary? You were just

a child. You needed only the coming
        morning to grow inside like the yellow

siren of the lilac. Like the voice that
        wants to escape you. I want to tell you

to run. To be safe. To forget your breaths
        will run out. To hold tight to your body

as if it is the only one you'll have.
        As if need is a door you won't open.

vi.

As if need is a door you won't open,

        you sleep in the room farthest from yourself.

You wake in a blue rain. You forget where

            you came from. You forget your name wasn't meant

for someone else. You forget the children

        you never had. You forget how you want

them even now. You tell no one. You tell

            no one how it is to be a woman

and living. You don't speak. You don't speak to

        the woman you called *mother.* You don't speak

to the last gasp when her body gave up.

            You don't say it hurts when you find her in-

side you. You leave her in the room farthest

        from the small fact of your heart, its shatter.

vii.

From the small fact of your heart, its shatter,
where did one woman end & one begin?
What paled like the tulip before winter

swept the branches bare of leaves? What became
the body? The flesh? The child? The hard-won
wound? Is the coming snow a sign that birds

will escape the white glare of the windows?
And what will time escape with? Our mouths.
Youth. The children. The witnesses that stand

as still as trees as our bodies flee us.
Mother, you couldn't stop shaking. I can't
stop to grieve. As women, we cannot grieve

light that barrels over fields to find us.
I stayed away until your body was—

After You Almost Died the First Time

I called your name to hear
a voice like yours echo
in the rime. I called myself back

from the lure of a man's hands, the beggar
moon caught in my throat.
I called you *mother.* Not *mama.*

Not *mom.* I created distance
in that one word. The hull
& husk of your lung, spooned out.

Lobe by lobe, I called breath
an enemy. I was called *orphan*
by agencies. My father already dead,

as you raised us alone. I called you *hero*
for a while, then *whore.* Then leaf
that can't return to the tree. Or maybe

that was me. I called the days gray
horses. I called it love
when moss overran the pines.

I called you through this animal
loneliness. I called you someone
I didn't want to be. I called you, yesterday,

to wish you a good day. The sparrows
forgetting themselves in the glare
of the windows. I called the day

forward to fold over our voices.
I called to say love is evidence
of all that you've kept alive.

Poem in the Shape of a Wish

The future,
The future, blued
The future, blued as
The future, blued as storm
The future, blued as storm, still
The future, blued as storm, still love
The future, blued as storm, still love is
The future, blued as storm, still love is all
The future, blued as storm, still love is all *I*
The future, blued as storm, still love is all *I* know
The future, blued as storm, still love is all *I* know of
The future, blued as storm, still love is all *I* know of being
The future, blued as storm, still love is all *I* know of being broken
The future, blued as storm, still love is all *I* know of being broken into
The future, blued as storm, still love is all *I* know of being broken into myth

Early One Morning, Words Were Missing

Yet, there was a river.
Fir trees lining the banks.
I went there to leave.
I went where no one could.
Scarce in my body, why was I crying.
The heart: a *blood clock*.
I let myself down.
In the depths.
In the depths of this winter.
In shame.
A forest has so many places to hide.
Oh, daughter: *love is what I was.*
It wasn't enough.
Those useless blue nights.
When that which seemed easy was hard.
Tell me: have you seen me in the future?
Chance means that we are free.
I had you to save me.
No.
I had you to forgive myself.
Like a tree in Dante's forest.
I had to break.
So I could speak.

Imperium

I dreamt I was a god last night, but I couldn't save anyone
from their suffering.

What good is power?

The roses are dying on their stems.

I am lonely. (There is no meaning in this.)

Monsters have sprung from the walls
of my heart—little machines, little with desire.

Time comes and goes, yet I am missing
somewhere in the back of my mind.

Did I not have parents once? Are they not the reason I know love?

My children ask for food, for water. I have little to offer.

Dear heart of hearts—what hides in me?

The trestles are overcome with mold and dirt.

My child cries because his body will not abide him, growing slow
and sluggish while we sit still. Instead,

we build boats from honeycombs to float on the lake among the geese.

There is no one around for miles. There is no sound but our own steps,
parting the grass.

The geese peck at a muskrat's head when it surfaces.

We have only ourselves to blame.

Infinitesimal Calculus

I tear my hair out in my sleep
and wake braided to light, bereft
of the world and the people I know. The mirror

insists I'm having a break-
down because I can't create a solution
to absence, though I've created for myself

a life. Since my mother disappeared from all surfaces,
I haven't trusted anything I can see myself
inside. She once told me *be careful*

not to hurt anyone with words,
but the tulips cry whenever I speak
and I am too tired to answer

when children cry from a night
in a past life. Who said growth isn't
divisive? I on one side of morning's argument,

my children on another. My mother,
unnamed on any marker. *Nothing I write is real,*
I once explained to her, separating myself

from my speakers. Who will write to her
when I'm not here? Who will write to forget her?
Lightning attacked the ground outside my window

last night. I woke alone, not understanding why
the yard had burned. Not understanding why
I was spared. The tile cold beneath my feet.

Errata

after Lisa Fay Coutley

When I say it started with power
lines that were buried

below ground, I mean the children
I want are missing. They can't be seen

without a microscope, yet even the shower
drain needs a respite from blood. I mean

the body is a basin I empty & empty
of birds. The word *woman* is stolen

from wife, not womb. *See: to own;*
to be owned. God only knows what I own

if nothing inside my body can be trusted.
The man I love lies inside the dark bend

between my past & future, where I've lived
as the city a thousand stoplights ago.

When I say I've been happy, I mean there
are some heroics I can muster,

& marriage might not be one of them. Somehow,
every city looks habitable in hindsight. Like winter,

as it squares off against time again
tonight. When I say I blame myself, I mean

the wind will not be held. I mean the wind chimes
silver with hurt. I mean I love what I can't have

as I love anything—full of greed, yet
unsteadily. See: the scattered horizon

of my heart. The flightless trees,
unbodied after the fall.

Antipastoral

I enter the meadow the seventh day after a tornado
passes by, a mountain in its teeth.

I want the rain. I want the rain
below ground with all this world has

refused. At night
the moon is one of many, but I look

no further than this one sky.
I topple the stones stacked in the saw

grass. I relieve the honeysuckles of their closed
eyes. Some days, I wander these glades

alone. Who blesses the rain? I mistake

the rough grasses for other ruins
I've loved. Still, I sleep on the sunporch,

count the matchsticks, light citronella
lanterns. At dawn, a gone lover

candles in my palm. Who is possible
without water & light?

The windows, like want, I open.
The sky spits. I feel, & I feel nothing.

I anoint myself with sky, & swallow.

Economic Theory

Canadian pennies cost 1.6 cents to manufacture, and the government
expects to save $11M a year by eliminating them.
—*THE ECONOMIST* (2013)

In a bare room in the mind, Midwest
        light filtering through wood slats
in the blinds, the snow falls like a world
        beginning, & I'm tempted to say I begin,
though I have failed to love myself. Out of fear,
        sense slips away like years. A man broke
his fists against the night on my skin, left
        only pennies in lieu of reparations. What value

does a thing retain after the people in power
        devalue it? I lived near the well with water
not clean enough to drink. Priceless, I came home
        from foreign lands when working
three jobs didn't allow me a life. Marriage:
        a country foreign to one's birth. Always,
a man had all the power when I was young,
        & didn't have any money for food. There

isn't a day in this life that I haven't gone
        hungry. But the quiet in my kids' mouths
means I'll work twice as hard to feed them
        full. The garden, under snow. Forever, breath
is an argument against failure. With Botox
        & heady songs. Other rituals, like leaving
a conflict region, a woman invests in
        by beginning. I'm tempted to say I begin.

Acknowledgments

Gratitude to the editors of the following journals where these poems first appeared, sometimes in a slightly different form:

American Poetry Review: "In America"; *Arts & Letters:* "Apophenia" and "Praxis"; *Burning House Press:* "After a Suicide"; *The Collagist:* "After-wars"; *Colorado Review:* "Because We Can Never Know All the Initial Conditions of a Complex System in Sufficient Detail, We Cannot Hope to Predict the Ultimate Fate of a Complex System" and "As Stars Burrow against My Ribs"; *Crab Creek Review:* "It's Possible Sex Is Elegy"; *Crab Orchard Review:* "It's Possible a Mother's Body Is Elegy" (nominated for a Pushcart Prize); *Diagram:* "In the Alcoholic's Apartment, a Time Machine"; *Diode:* "Litany of When," "I Remember, I Remember," and "Topology"; *Epiphany:* "While Reading Plato during a Lockdown"; *Four Way Review:* "Memorial Day" and "Here, the Sparrows Were, All Along" (also published by Academy of American Poets); *Greensboro Review:* "No One Can Tell the Bones of the Dead from the Bones of the Living" (also published on Verse Daily); *Guernica:* "Notes on Inheritance"; *Harpur Palate:* "Noli Me Tangere"; *HocTok:* "Winter Solstice" and "Economic Theory"; *Iowa Review:* "Peripeteia"; *Kenyon Review Online:* "Principles of Chaos"; *Los Angeles Review:* "Psychogeography" (also the winner of the 2019 Margaret Reid Prize for poetry by Winning Writers); *Love's Executive Order:* "When the Right to Life Isn't a Right"; *Michigan Quarterly Review:* "Things I Never Give Myself Permission to Say"; *Narrative Northeast:* "After You Almost Died the First Time"; *Nashville Review:* "At the Brain Injury Research Institute" and "Complex Nonlinear Systems"; *New England Review:* "Antipastoral"; *New Republic:* "Postliminium"; *The Puritan:* "You Were Found in the Belly of a Deer Once" (winner of the 2019 Thomas Morton Prize in poetry); *Quarterly West:* "Powerlessness Is the Animal We Fear" and "Diagnoses"; *Redivider:* "On Traumatic Brain Injury"; *The Rumpus:* "Springbank" and "Shapeshifting"; *Salt Hill:* "A Name for Illness I Knew, but Couldn't Say" (also published on Verse Daily); *The Shallow Ends:* "From Nashville, I Revisit the Days I Lived in Vancouver"; *Southern Review:* "& What if I Spoke of the Hours,"

"Epistemology," and "An Incomplete Chronology" (also published by Academy of American Poets); *Sugar House Review:* "Doppelgänger" and "At the Insight Ultrasound Lab for a Breast Cancer Screening after the Mammogram Finds Irregularities"; *TriQuarterly:* "Marcescence"; *Waxwing:* "Errata" and "As Safe as Night"; *West Review:* "Occupation," "Even in an Emergency," and "When the Wind Culls Its Name"; *Wildness:* "Of Those Who Can't Afford to Be Gentle."

Thank you also to *The Slowdown* & its host, Ada Limón, for featuring my poem "Complex Nonlinear Systems" on the podcast in January 2022.

I am reminded that this work is not possible without the generosity of others. That I wrote this during a global pandemic, at a time when people were dying rapidly in isolation, when people I knew & loved were living with cancer & alcoholism & depression & brain injury & other diseases, only made these poems more urgent. I am indebted to the people who taught me that the questions worth asking are often those without answers.

Thank you, Jay Hopler, for your time when it grew short; for "getting out of my way," as you put it; for rigorously expanding my ideas of the poem and what is possible; for teaching me to hear. You were alive when I wrote these poems— they began in your classroom, where I last saw you. Perhaps my poems will forever begin there. Words fail me when I try to explain the gifts you've given me. I hope to make you proud, always.

Thank you, John A. Nieves. To writing poems that care. You are the best. I couldn't do any of this without you. Your generosity amazes & inspires me, as do your poems.

To Nancy Reddy for helping clarify the ambitions of this collection at a time when I really needed it. Thank you—for everything.

Thank you to Heather Sellers for your care & advice; that it is ongoing, I am grateful.

Thank you to James Long & LSU Press for believing in this work. I am thrilled to be part of your publishing family.

Thank you to my children, my husband, & our families. I love you.

Thank you to those teachers who take the time, who make all the difference in their students' lives, who lead with generosity, curiosity, & care. It only takes one teacher to change a child's life, & I'm lucky that I've had great teachers in mine.

We will pay forward someone else's kindness forever, if we're lucky enough, I wrote recently to a friend. I aspire to be that lucky. Thank you: poems, readers, & friends. All my love & gratitude.

Notes

Epigraph I is taken from the research article "A History of Chaos Theory," by Christian Oestreicher, published in *Dialogues in Clinical Neuroscience* (2007).

Epigraph II is a well-known quote from Edward Norton Lorenz, an MIT professor who is considered the official discoverer of chaos theory. The quote was coined by Philip E. Merilees, a meteorologist who organized a 1972 convention where Lorenz gave a lecture on chaos theory. It was Merilees who named the lecture: "Predictability: Does the Flap of a Butterfly's Wing in Brazil Cause a Tornado in Texas?"

"Fractals": the epigraph is a quote by Albert Einstein, borrowed from an article at the fractalfoundation.org.

"Strange Attractors": the title and the epigraph are borrowed from "Conclusion: What Creativity Is and Is Not," in *Creativity: Theories and Themes: Research, Development, and Practice,* edited by Mark Runco (2014). The quote itself is attributed to researcher James Gleick.

"At the Brain Injury Research Institute": the italicized line is from the long poem "Training Camp: Deer Lake, PA," by Gabrielle Calvocoressi, from the collection *Apocalyptic Swing Poems* (2009).

"No One Can Tell the Bones of the Dead from the Bones of the Living": the title is borrowed from *The Half-Finished Heaven*, by Tomas Tranströmer (2001).

"Of Those Who Can't Afford to Be Gentle": the title and the italicized lines are from the essay "Of Those Who Can Afford to Be Gentle I'll say it again," by C. D. Wright, from *The Poet, the Lion, Talking Pictures, El Farolito, a Wedding in St. Roch, the Big Box Store, the Warp in the Mirror, Spring, Midnights, Fire & All* (2016).

"Because We Can Never Know All the Initial Conditions of a Complex System in Sufficient Detail, We Cannot Hope to Predict the Ultimate Fate of a Complex System": the title is borrowed from an article on chaos theory at fractalfoundation.org.

"I Remember, I Remember": the premise of the poem is borrowed from the essay of the same name by Mary Ruefle, published in *Madness, Rack, and Honey: Collected Lectures* (2012).

"After a Suicide": the italicized lines refer to the long poem *Please Bury Me in This*, by Allison Benis White (2017).

"Things I Never Give Myself Permission to Say": the italicized line refers to the poem "Yellow Stars and Ice," by Susan Stewart, from the collection *Yellow Stars and Ice* (1981).

"A Name for Illness I Knew but Couldn't Say": the poem jumps off from, and is in conversation with, "River Pilgrims," by Jennifer Chang, from *Some Say the Lark* (2017).

"It's Possible a Mother's Body Is Elegy" is for my mother-in-law, Darlene Dingman, who died of cancer in August 2017.

"Errata" borrows from, and is in conversation with, "Errata," by Lisa Fay Coutley, from *Errata* (2015).

"Economic Theory": the epigraph is taken from a 2013 article in *The Economist* by L. M. entitled, "Why Has Canada Killed Off the Penny?"

Printed in the USA
CPSIA information can be obtained
at www.ICGtesting.com
LVHW090415160923
758324LV00003B/403